Contents

THAI STYLE BROCCOLI MIX

Prep Time: 10 mins - **Total Time:** 30 mins

SERVINGS: 4

NUTRITIONAL VALUE

Calories 315 kcal, Carbohydrates 8.2 g, Cholesterol 65 mg, Fat 18.9 g, Fiber 3.2 g, Protein 28.3 g, Sodium 275 mg

INGREDIENTS

- 2 tbsps olive oil
- 1/2 cup peanut sauce (such as House of
- 2 large skinless, boneless chicken breast
- Tsang®), or to taste
- halves, cut into bite-size pieces
- 1 pinch salt to taste
- 1 (12 ounce) package broccoli coleslaw mix
- 1 tsp sesame oil, or to taste
- 1/2 cup water

DIRECTIONS

Step 1

Cook chicken in hot olive oil for about 5 minutes before you add water, broccoli and sesame oil.

Step 2

Cook this on medium heat for about 15 minutes or until you see that the broccoli slaw is tender.

Step 3

Do add some peanut sauce and salt according to your taste before serving.

THAI **CUCUMBER SOUP**

Prep Time: 15 mins - **Total Time:** 45 mins

SERVINGS: 4

NUTRITIONAL VALUE

Calories 67 kcal, Carbohydrates 6.8 g, Cholesterol 3 mg, Fat 4 g, Fiber 1.4 g, Protein 1.7 g, Sodium 702 mg

INGREDIENTS

- 1 tbsp vegetable oil
- 3 cucumbers, peeled and diced
- 1/2 cup chopped green onion
- 2 1/2 cups chicken broth
- 1 1/2 tbsps lemon juice
- 1 tsp white sugar
- salt and ground black pepper to taste

DIRECTIONS

Step 1

Cook cucumber in hot olive oil for about 5 minutes before adding green onions and cooking for another five minutes.

Step 2

Add chicken broth, sugar and lemon juice into it before bringing all this to boil.

Step 3

Turn down the heat to low and cook for another 20 minutes before adding salt and black pepper according to your taste.

Step 4

Serve.

CHARONG'S **GINGER SOUP**

Prep Time: 15 mins **- Total Time:** 25 mins

SERVINGS: 4

NUTRITIONAL VALUE

Calories 415 kcal, Carbohydrates 7.3 g, Cholesterol 29 mg, Fat 39 g, Fiber 2.1 g, Protein 14.4 g, Sodium 598 mg

INGREDIENTS

- 3 cups coconut milk
- 1/4 cup fresh lime juice
- 2 cups water
- 2 tbsps sliced green onions
- 1/2 pound skinless, boneless chicken
- 1 tbsp chopped fresh cilantro
- breast halves - cut into thin strips
- 3 tbsps minced fresh ginger root
- 2 tbsps fish sauce, or to taste

DIRECTIONS

Step 1

Bring the mixture of coconut milk and water to boil before adding chicken strips, and cooking it for three minutes on medium heat or until you see that the chicken is cooked through.

Step 2

Now add ginger, green onions, lime juice, cilantro and fish sauce into it.

Step 3

Mix it well and serve.

THAI BBQ CHICKEN

Prep Time: 15 mins - **Total Time:** 4 hrs 15 mins

SERVINGS: 4

NUTRITIONAL VALUE

Calories 564 kcal, Carbohydrates 52.4 g, Cholesterol 230 mg, Fat 19.3 g, Fiber 4.3 g, Protein 46.3 g, Sodium 375 mg

INGREDIENTS

- 1 bunch fresh cilantro with roots
- 3 tbsps fish sauce
- 3 cloves garlic, peeled
- 1 (3 pound) chicken, cut into pieces
- 3 small red hot chili peppers, seeded and
- 1/4 cup coconut milk
- chopped
- 1 tsp ground turmeric
- 1 tsp curry powder
- 1 tbsp white sugar
- 1 pinch salt

DIRECTIONS

Step 1

At first you need to set a grill or grilling plate to medium heat and put some oil before starting anything else.

Step 2

Put minced cilantro roots, salt, leaves, chili peppers, curry powder, turmeric, sugar, fish sauce, garlic in a blender and blend until you see that the required smoothness is achieved.

Step 3

Combine this paste and chicken in large bowl, and refrigerate it for at least three hours for margination.

Step 4

Cook this on the preheated grill for about 15 minutes each side or until tender, while brushing it regularly with coconut milk.

Step 5

Serve.

THAI CHICKEN CURRY II

Prep Time: 15 mins - **Total Time:** 35 mins

SERVINGS: 4

NUTRITIONAL VALUE

Calories 621 kcal, Carbohydrates 86.7 g, Cholesterol 91 mg, Fat 19.4 g, Fiber 2.1 g, Protein 35.2 g, Sodium 316 mg

INGREDIENTS

- 1 tbsp canola oil
- 1/4 cup milk
- 2 tbsps green curry paste
- 1/8 tsp white pepper
- 1 pound boneless skinless chicken
- 2 cups hot cooked long-grain white
- breasts, cut into bite-size pieces

- rice
- 1 small onion, thinly sliced
- 1 red pepper, cut into thin strips, then
- cut crosswise in half
- 1 green pepper, cut into thin strips, then
- cut crosswise in half
- 4 ounces cream cheese, cubed

DIRECTIONS

Step 1

Combine curry paste and hot oil before adding chicken and onions.

Step 2

Cook this for about 8 minutes before adding green and red peppers, and cooking for another five minutes.

Step 3

Now add cream cheese, white pepper and milk, and cook until you see that the cheese has melted.

Step 4

Serve this on top of rice.

Step 5

Enjoy.

THAI CHICKEN CURRY

Prep Time: 15 mins - **Total Time:** 55 mins

SERVINGS: 6

NUTRITIONAL VALUE

Calories 500 kcal, Carbohydrates 22.1 g, Cholesterol 58 mg, Fat 36.1 g, Fiber 3.6 g, Protein 25.8 g, Sodium 437 mg

INGREDIENTS

- 1 tbsp olive oil
- 3 small red potatoes, cut into cubes, or as
- 3 tbsps Thai yellow curry paste (such as needed Mae Ploy®)
- 3 red Thai chili peppers, chopped with seeds, 1 pound cooked skinless, boneless or more to taste chicken breast, cut into bite-size pieces
- 1 tsp fish sauce
- 2 (14 ounce) cans coconut milk
- 1 cup chicken stock
- 1 yellow onion, chopped

DIRECTIONS

Step 1

Mix curry paste in hot oil before adding chicken and coating it well.

Step 2

Add 1 can coconut milk and cook it for five minutes before adding the rest of the coconut milk, onion, potatoes, chicken stock and chili peppers into it and bringing all this to boil.

Step 3

Turn the heat down to low and cook for 25 minutes or until the potatoes are tender.

Step 4

Add fish sauce into before serving.

Step 5

Enjoy..

JAPANESE RUSSET CURRY

Prep Time: 10 mins - **Total Time:** 25 mins

SERVINGS: 4

NUTRITIONAL VALUE

Calories 292.4, Fat 9.0g , Cholesterol 0.0mg , Sodium 57.8mg , Carbohydrates 50.3g , Protein 9.9g

INGREDIENTS

- 2 tbsp oil
- 1 1/2 C. chicken
- 1 onion, diced
- 1 large russet potato, peeled, in bite-size cubes
- 1 head broccoli, cut into small pieces
- 1 (14 1/2 oz) cans baby corn, cut in half
- 1 (3 1/2 oz) boxes golden curry sauce mix

DIRECTIONS

Step 1

Place a soup pot over medium heat. Heat the oil in it. Cook it in the chicken with onion for 5 min.

Step 2

Add the potato with 2 3/4 C. of water. Put on the lid and lower the heat. Cook them for 12 min. Crumble the curry sauce mix and stir it until it melts for 3 min.

Step 3

Stir in the corn with broccoli. Cook the stew for 4 min. Serve it warm.

Step 4

Enjoy.

JAPANESE **CHICKEN THIGHS SKILLET**

Prep Time: 10 mins - **Total Time:** 30 mins

SERVINGS: 4

NUTRITIONAL VALUE

Calories 128.4, Fat 7.2g , Cholesterol 39.4mg , Sodium 585.9mg , Carbohydrates 6.1g , Protein 9.6g

INGREDIENTS

- 2 -3 boneless chicken thighs
- 8 fresh shiitake mushrooms
- 8 shishito green peppers or 3 small bell peppers
- 2 -3 tbsp mirin
- 2 -3 tbsp soy sauce
- japanese sansho pepper (optional)
- shichimi togarashi pepper or red chili
- pepper flakes (optional)

DIRECTIONS

Step 1

Discard the fat from the chicken. Discard the mushroom tips and cut them into quarters.

Step 2

Remove the bell peppers stems and cut them into bite size pieces.

Step 3

Place a large skillet over medium heat. Grease it with some oil. Cook in it the chicken thighs with the skin facing down until it becomes crisp and golden brown.

Step 4

Stir in the pepper with mushroom. Flip the chicken thighs and cook them on the other side until they become golden brown.

Step 5

Stir in the mirin with soy sauce. Cook them until they sauce becomes thick, the chicken and veggies done. Serve your chicken skillet warm.

Step 6

Enjoy.

SOON DU BU JIGAE TOFU STEW

Prep Time: 5 mins - **Total Time:** 20 mins

SERVINGS: 2

NUTRITIONAL VALUE

Calories 242 kcal, Fat 16.5 g, Carbohydrates 7g, Protein 20 g, Cholesterol 99 mg, Sodium 415 mg

INGREDIENTS

- 1 tsp vegetable oil
- 1 tsp sesame seeds
- 1 tsp Korean chile powder
- 1 green onion, diced
- 2 tbsps ground beef (optional)
- 1 tbsp Korean soy bean paste
- (doenjang)

- 1 C. water
- salt and pepper to taste
- 1 (12 oz.) package Korean soon tofu or
- soft tofu, drained and sliced
- 1 egg

DIRECTIONS

Step 1

Stir fry your beef and chili powder in veggie oil until the beef is fully done then add the bean paste and stir.

Step 2

Now add in the water and get everything boiling before adding in some pepper and salt.

Step 3

Once the mix is boiling add in your tofu and cook the contents for 4 mins.

Step 4

Shut the heat and crack your egg into the soup.

Step 5

Stir everything and let the egg poach before adding a garnishing of green onions and sesame seeds.

Step 6

Enjoy.

KOREAN PIZZAS

Prep Time: 10 mins - **Total Time:** 40 mins

SERVINGS: 8

NUTRITIONAL VALUE

Calories 233 kcal, Fat 7 g, Carbohydrates 30.1g, Protein 12.7 g, Cholesterol 3 mg, Sodium 663 mg

INGREDIENTS

- 2 C. all-purpose flour
- 1/2 C. shredded cabbage
- 2 eggs
- 4 tsps canola oil
- 4 C. water
- 1/4 C. soy sauce
- 1/2 tsp salt
- 2 tbsps rice vinegar
- 1 shallot, diced
- 1 tbsp sesame oil
- 1 green onion, diced
- 1 chili pepper, diced (optional)
- 1/2 C. minced crabmeat
- 1/2 C. diced cooked pork
- 1/2 C. diced firm tofu
- 1 C. bean sprouts
- 1 C. frozen mixed vegetables, thawed

DIRECTIONS

Step 1

Get a bowl, combine: chili pepper, soy sauce, sesame oil, and vinegar. Place this mix to the side.

Step 2

Get a 2nd bowl, combine: salt, flour, water, and eggs. Now add the: cabbage, crabmeat, mixed veggies, pork, sprouts, and tofu.

Step 3

Now it is important that you get your oil very in a skillet then add in enough of the batter to coat the bottom of the pan.

Step 4

Let this fry for 9 mins then flip it and cook for 4 more mins.

Step 5

Continue with all of the remaining mix.

Step 6

Finally top your dish with some of the sauce.

Step 7

Enjoy.

TUNA AND RICE (CHOMPCHAE DEOPBAP)

Prep Time: 10 mins - **Total Time:** 50 mins

SERVINGS: 2

NUTRITIONAL VALUE

Calories 562 kcal, Fat 9 g, Carbohydrates 87.5g, Protein 31.8 g, Cholesterol 25 mg, Sodium 1507 mg

INGREDIENTS

- 1 C. uncooked white rice
- 2 tbsps rice vinegar
- 2 C. water

- salt and pepper to taste
- 1 tbsp olive oil
- 1 tbsp Korean chili powder, or to
- 3 cloves garlic, minced taste
- 1 (1/2 inch) piece fresh ginger, minced
- 1 tbsp water, or as needed
- 1/2 onion, coarsely diced
- 1 (6 oz.) can tuna, drained
- 1 C. kim chee
- 1/2 C. sliced cucumber
- 1/4 C. sliced carrots
- 2 tbsps soy sauce

DIRECTIONS

Step 1

Get your rice boiling with 2 C. of water, once it is boiling place a lid on the pot, set the hea to low, and let it cook for 23 mins.

Step 2

Stir fry your onions, ginger, and garlic in olive oil for 7 mins then add in: vinegar, carrots, soy sauce, pepper, salt, chili powder, cucumbers, and kimchee.

Step 3

Cook and add in your tuna, while stirring until everything is hot.

Step 4

Layer the rice with a topping of tuna mix on each plate.

Step 5

Enjoy.

KOREAN **BURRITOS**

Prep Time: 15 mins - **Total Time:** 30 mins

SERVINGS: 4

NUTRITIONAL VALUE

Calories 597 kcal, Fat 29.1 g, Carbohydrates 45.6g, Protein 38.5 g, Cholesterol 97 mg, Sodium 1635 mg

INGREDIENTS

- 2 tsps butter, softened (optional)
- 6 cloves garlic, minced
- 1 C. fresh cilantro leaves
- 2 tbsps Korean chili paste (gochujang)
- 1/2 C. diced kimchi, squeezed dry
- 1 tbsp soy sauce
- 2 tsps white sugar
- 2 tbsps shredded sharp Cheddar
- 1 tsp sesame oil cheese
- 2 (10 oz.) cans chicken chunks, drained
- 1 tbsp salsa
- Everything Else:
- 4 (10 inch) flour tortillas
- 2 tbsps vegetable oil

DIRECTIONS

Step 1

Set your oven to 350 degrees before doing anything else.

Step 2

Get a bowl, combine: sesame oil, garlic, sugar, soy sauce, and chili paste. Then add the chicken and stir everything.

Step 3

Cover your tortillas with some foil and cook them for 12 mins in the oven.

Step 4

At the same time begin to stir fry your chicken in veggie oil with the marinade.

Step 5

Cook the chicken for about 12 mins as well.

Step 6

Coat each tortilla with half a tsp of butter then add an equal amount of chicken to each.

Step 7

Add the following to each tortilla before folding: salsa, cilantro, cheddar, and kimchi.

Step 8

Shape everything into tacos and serve.

Step 9

Enjoy.

KOREAN BURRITOS KOREAN SHORT RIBS II

Prep Time: 20 mins - **Total Time:** 1 hr 20 mins

SERVINGS: 6

NUTRITIONAL VALUE

Calories 647 kcal, Fat 54.9 g, Carbohydrates 14.1g, Protein 23.3 g, Cholesterol 115 mg, Sodium 805 mg

INGREDIENTS

- 2 lbs beef short ribs, trimmed
- 1/4 C. brown sugar
- 1 green onion, diced
- 2 C. water to cover
- 2 carrots, peeled and diced
- 4 cloves garlic, minced
- 1 (1 inch) piece fresh ginger root, diced
- 1/2 C. reduced-sodium soy sauce

DIRECTIONS

Step 1

Cut some incisions into your beef then add them into a pan with: brown sugar, green onions, soy sauce, carrots, ginger, and garlic.

Step 2

Add in some water to cover the contents and get everything boiling.

Step 3

Once it is all boiling set the heat to low and let the contents cook for 60 mins.

Step 4

Remove any excess oils then plate the contents.

Step 5

Enjoy.

YAKI MANDU KOREAN EGG ROLLS

Prep Time: 30 mins - **Total Time:** 45 mins

SERVINGS: 25

NUTRITIONAL VALUE

Calories 125 kcal, Fat 5.8 g, Carbohydrates 12.1g, Protein 5.7 g, Cholesterol 28 mg, Sodium 246 mg

INGREDIENTS

- 1 lb ground beef
- salt and ground black pepper to taste
- 1 1/2 C. vegetable oil for frying
- 2 eggs
- 1/2 C. finely diced green onions
- 1 (16 oz.) package wonton wrappers
- 1/2 C. finely diced cabbage
- 3 tbsps soy sauce
- 1/2 C. finely diced carrot
- 2 tsps rice wine vinegar
- 1/2 C. minced garlic
- 1 tsp toasted sesame seeds, or more
- 4 tsps sesame oil, divided to taste
- 1 tbsp toasted sesame seeds
- 1/2 tsp monosodium glutamate (such as Ac'cent(R))

DIRECTIONS

Step 1

Stir fry your beef for 8 mins.

Step 2

At the same time in another pot for 12 mins cook: ground beef, green onions, pepper, cabbage, salt, carrots, MSG, garlic, 1 tbsp of sesame oil and seeds. Then remove everything from the pan.

Step 3

Coat a wonton wrapper with some whisked egg and then add 1 tsp of beef mix into it.

Step 4

Then fold everything into a triangle and crimp the edges.

Step 5

Do this for all your ingredients.

Step 6

Then for 3 mins per side fry the wontons then place layer them on some paper towels.

Step 7

Get a bowl, combine: 1 tsp sesame seeds, soy sauce, 1 tsp sesame oil, and vinegar.

Step 8

Use this as topping for your wontons.

Step 9

Enjoy.

KOREAN CURRY

Prep Time: 20 mins - **Total Time:** 1 hr 20 mins

SERVINGS: 6

NUTRITIONAL VALUE

Calories 303 kcal, Fat 13.6 g, Carbohydrates 27.9g, Protein 17.6 g, Cholesterol 36 mg, Sodium 60 mg

INGREDIENTS

- 1/4 C. olive oil, divided
- 1 tbsp Korean-style curry powder (such as
- 1 1/2 lbs boneless chicken breast, cut into Assi(R) mild curry powder), or more to taste cubes
- 1 large yellow onion, cut into cubes
- 2 large russet potatoes, peeled and cut into cubes
- 3 large carrots, peeled and cut into cubes
- 4 C. water

DIRECTIONS

Step 1

Stir fry your chicken in 2 tbsps of olive oil for about 13 mins or until fully done.

Step 2

Then in another pot stir fry your carrots, potatoes, and onions in more olive oil for 8 mins.

Step 3

Add the chicken to the veggies and add some water.

Step 4

Place a lid on the pot and let the contents gently boil for 22 mins.

Step 5

Shut the heat and add in your curry and stir everything until the spice is completely mixed in.

Step 6

Now cook everything for 25 more mins until the sauce is thick.

Step 7

Enjoy.

CHICKEN STEW KOREAN

Prep Time: 20 mins - **Total Time:** 1 hr 5 mins

SERVINGS: 4

NUTRITIONAL VALUE

Calories 896 kcal, Fat 69.1 g, Carbohydrates 136.1g, Protein 33.4 g, Cholesterol 121 mg, Sodium 1111 mg

INGREDIENTS

1 1/2 C. water, Fat and cut into small pieces

- 1/4 C. soy sauce
- 10 oz. potatoes, cut into large chunks
- 2 tbsps rice wine
- 2 carrots, cut into large chunks
- 2 tbsps Korean red chili pepper paste
- 1/2 large onion, cut into large chunks
- (gochujang)
- 4 large garlic cloves, or more to taste
- 2 tbsps Korean red chili pepper flakes
- 2 slices fresh ginger, or more to taste
- (gochugaru)
- 2 scallions, cut into 2-inch lengths
- 1 tbsp honey
- 1 tbsp sesame oil

- 1 tbsp white sugar
- 1 tsp sesame seeds
- 1 pinch ground black pepper
- 3 lbs bone-in chicken pieces, trimmed of

DIRECTIONS

Step 1

Get the following boiling in a big pot: chicken, water, black pepper, soy sauce, sugar, wine, honey, pepper paste, and pepper flakes.

Step 2

Once everything is boiling set the heat to low and place a lid on the pot.

Step 3

Let the contents cook for 17 mins.

Step 4

Add in: ginger, potatoes, garlic, carrots, and onions and cook the mix for 17 more mins.

Step 5

Take off the lid and continue cooking for 12 more mins.

Step 6

Now add in some sesame seeds, scallions, and sesame oil.

Step 7

Enjoy.

HOW TO MAKE KIMCHEE

Prep Time: 30 mins - **Total Time:** 3 days 3 hrs

SERVINGS: 30

NUTRITIONAL VALUE

Calories 6 kcal, Fat < 0 g, Carbohydrates < 1.5g, Protein < 0.3 g, Cholesterol < 0 mg, Sodium 932 mg

INGREDIENTS

- 1 head Napa cabbage, cubed
- 1 small radish, shredded
- 1/4 C. salt, divided
- 1 cucumber, diced (optional)
- 6 cloves garlic
- 1 (1 inch) piece fresh ginger root, peeled and diced
- 1 small white onion, peeled and diced
- 2 tbsps water
- 3 green onions, mincedcayenne pepper to taste
- 1 ripe persimmon, diced

DIRECTIONS

Step 1

Get a bowl and combine your cabbage and salt.

Step 2

Let it sit for 60 mins then add in more salt and let it stand for 60 more mins.

Step 3

Now remove all the liquids and wash the leaves off.

Step 4

Now blend the following until paste-like: onions, ginger, and garlic.

Step 5

Add this to the cabbage along with: cucumbers, green onions, persimmon, cayenne, and radishes.

Step 6

Place a covering on the bowl and let it sit in the fridge for at least 2 days.

Step 7

Enjoy.

KOREAN EGG ROLLS II

Prep Time: 45 mins - **Total Time:** 1 hr

SERVINGS: 6

NUTRITIONAL VALUE

Calories 534 kcal, Fat 28.4 g, Carbohydrates 56.9g, Protein 14.6 g, Cholesterol 67 mg, Sodium 1177 mg

INGREDIENTS

- 1/2 (8 oz.) package dry thin Asian rice
- 2 tsps salt
- noodles (rice vermicelli)
- 1 (12 oz.) package round wonton wrappers
- 1/2 medium head cabbage, cored and
- 1/2 C. vegetable oil for frying shredded
- 1 (12 oz.) package firm tofu
- 2 small zucchini, shredded
- 4 green onions, finely diced
- 4 cloves garlic, finely diced
- 1 tbsp ground black pepper

- 2 tbsps Asian (toasted) sesame oil
- 2 eggs, slightly beaten

DIRECTIONS

Step 1

Boil your noodles in water for 6 mins. Then remove all the liquids and run them under cold water.

Step 2

Now dice the noodles and place everything to the side.

Step 3

Squeeze your cabbage to drain any liquids and place them in a bowl with: noodles, tofu, salt, zucchini, eggs, sesame oil, green onions, black pepper, and garlic.

Step 4

Mix everything with your hands and try to break up your tofu pieces.

Step 5

Add 2 tsp of mix into your wonton wrappers and coat the edge with some water before shaping the wrapper into a triangle and crimping the edges.

Step 6

Continue for all your ingredients then fry the wontons in veggie oil for 4 mins per side.

Step 7

Enjoy.

KOREAN **SUSHI**

Prep Time: 40 mins - **Total Time:** 1 hr

SERVINGS: 4

NUTRITIONAL VALUE

Calories 354 kcal, Fat 15.2 g, Carbohydrates 41.2g, Protein 11.9 g, Cholesterol 113 mg, Sodium 510 mg

INGREDIENTS

- 1 C. uncooked glutinous white rice into thin strips (sushi rice)
- 4 slices cooked ham, cut into thin
- 1 1/2 C. water strips, optional
- 1 tbsp sesame oil
- 2 tsps sesame oil
- salt, to taste
- 2 eggs, beaten
- 4 sheets sushi nori (dry seaweed)
- 1 cucumber, cut into thin strips
- 1 carrot, cut into thin strips
- 4 slices American processed cheese, cut

DIRECTIONS

Step 1

Get your water and rice boiling.

Step 2

Once it is boiling, place a lid on the pot, and set the heat to low.

Step 3

Let the rice cook for 15 mins.

Step 4

Now pour the rice into a casserole dish to lose its heat.

Step 5

At same time as the rice is cooking fry your eggs without stirring.

Step 6

Place your nori sheet on a counter top and layer each with an equal amount of rice.

Step 7

Now layer: ham, egg, cucumbers, cheese, and carrots.

Step 8

Roll up the sheet with a bamboo mat and top each with half a tsp of sesame oil.

Step 9

Dice up the roll into 6 pieces of sushi.

Step 10

Enjoy.

CHAP CHEE NOODLES

Prep Time: 35 mins **- Total Time:** 1 hr

SERVINGS: 4

NUTRITIONAL VALUE

Calories 264 kcal, Fat 12.5 g, Carbohydrates 27.9g, Protein 10.6 g, Cholesterol 23 mg, Sodium 1025 mg

INGREDIENTS

- 1 tbsp soy sauce
- 1/4 lb napa cabbage, sliced
- 1 tbsp sesame oil
- 2 C. diced fresh spinach
- 2 green onions, finely diced

- 3 oz. cellophane noodles, soaked in warm
- 1 clove garlic, minced
- water
- 1 tsp sesame seeds
- 2 tbsps soy sauce
- 1 tsp sugar
- 1 tbsp sugar
- 1/4 tsp black pepper
- 1/2 tsp salt
- 1/3 lb beef top sirloin, thinly sliced
- 1/4 tsp black pepper
- 2 tbsps vegetable oil
- 1/2 C. thinly sliced carrots
- 1/2 C. sliced bamboo shoots, drained

DIRECTIONS

Step 1

Get a bowl, combine: a quarter of a C. of pepper, 1 tbsp of soy sauce, 1 tsp of sugar, sesame oil, sesame seeds, garlic, and green onions. Add in the beef and let the content sit for 17 mins.

Step 2

Now stir fry the beef in oil until fill done then add in: spinach, carrots, cabbage, and bamboo. Cook for 2 more mins before add in: quarter tsp of pepper, half a tsp salt, 1 tbsps sugar, 2 tbsps of soy sauce, and noodles.

Step 3

Set the heat to low and heat all the contents up.

Step 4

Enjoy.

GALBI KOREAN SHORT RIBS III

Prep Time: 1 hr - **Total Time:** 10 hrs

SERVINGS: 6

NUTRITIONAL VALUE

Calories 1092 kcal, Fat 78.6 g, Carbohydrates 157.5g, Protein 39.1 g, Cholesterol 155 mg, Sodium 2501 mg

INGREDIENTS

- 5 lbs beef short ribs, cut flanken style
- 5 cloves garlic
- 1 onion, coarsely diced
- 1 Asian pear, cored and cubed
- 1 C. soy sauce (such as Kikkoman(R))
- 1 C. brown sugar
- 1/4 C. honey
- 1/4 C. sesame oil

black pepper to taste

DIRECTIONS

Step 1

Submerge your ribs in water for 60 mins then then drain them.

Step 2

Puree the following in a blender: pear, onions, and garlic. Add this to a bowl with: black pepper, soy sauce, sesame oil, brown sugar, and honey. Place your ribs in the mix and let it sit in the fridge for 8 hrs with a covering of plastic.

Step 3

Now grill your beef on an oiled grate for 7 mins per side.

Step 4

Enjoy.

FRESH **THAI PESTO**

Prep Time: 10 mins - **Total Time:** 10 mins

SERVINGS: 12

NUTRITIONAL VALUE

Calories 84 kcal, Carbohydrates 3.4 g, Cholesterol 0 mg, Fat 7.4 g, Fiber 0.6 g, Protein 1.9 g, Sodium 197 mg

INGREDIENTS

- 1 bunch cilantro
- 1/4 cup peanut butter
- 3 cloves garlic, minced
- 3 tbsps extra-virgin olive oil
- 2 tbsps minced fresh ginger
- 1 1/2 tbsps fish sauce
- 1 tbsp brown sugar
- 1/2 tsp cayenne pepper

DIRECTIONS

Step 1

Put all the ingredients that are mentioned above in a blender and blend it until you see that the required smoothness is achieved.

CLASSICAL PAD THAI NOODLES I

Prep Time: 35 mins - **Total Time:** 2 hrs

SERVINGS: 4

NUTRITIONAL VALUE

Calories 397 kcal, Carbohydrates 39.5 g, Cholesterol 41 mg, Fat 23.3 g, Fiber 5 g, Protein 13.2 g, Sodium 1234 mg

INGREDIENTS

- 2/3 cup dried rice vermicelli
- 3 tbsps chopped peanuts
- 1/4 cup peanut oil
- 1 pound bean sprouts, divided
- 2/3 cup thinly sliced firm tofu
- 3 green onions, whites cut thinly across and 1 large egg, beaten
- greens sliced into thin lengths - divided
- 4 cloves garlic, finely chopped
- 3 tbsps chopped peanuts
- 1/4 cup vegetable broth
- 2 limes, cut into wedges for garnish
- 2 tbsps fresh lime juice
- 2 tbsps soy sauce
- 1 tbsp white sugar
- 1 tsp salt
- 1/2 tsp dried red chili flakes

DIRECTIONS

Step 1

Put rice vermicelli noodles in hot water for about 30 minutes before draining the water.

Step 2

Cook tofu in hot oil until golden brown before draining it with paper tower.

Step 3

Reserve 1 tbsp of oil for later use and cook egg in the remaining hot oil until done, and set them aside for later use.

Step 4

Now cook noodles and garlic in the hot reserved oil, while coating them well with this oil along the way.

Step 5

In this pan containing noodles; add tofu, salt, chili flakes, egg and 3 tbsps peanuts, and mix all this very thoroughly.

Step 6

Also add bean sprouts and green onion into it, while reserving some for the garnishing purposes.

Step 7

Cook all this for two minutes before transferring to a serving platter.

Step 8

Garnish this with peanuts and the reserved vegetables before placing some lime wedges around the platter to make this dish more attractive.

Step 9

Serve.

CLASSICAL **PAD THAI NOODLE II**

Prep Time: 15 mins - **Total Time:** 25 mins

SERVINGS: 4

NUTRITIONAL VALUE

Calories 352 kcal, Carbohydrates 46.8 g, Cholesterol 46 mg, Fat 15 g, Fiber 3 g, Protein 9.2 g, Sodium 335 mg

INGREDIENTS

- 1 (6.75 ounce) package thin rice noodles
- 1 tbsp chopped fresh cilantro
- 2 tbsps vegetable oil
- 1 lime, cut into wedges
- 3 ounces fried tofu, sliced into thin strips
- 1 clove garlic, minced
- 1 egg
- 1 tbsp soy sauce
- 1 pinch white sugar
- 2 tbsps chopped peanuts
- 1 cup fresh bean sprouts

DIRECTIONS

Step 1

In a heatproof bowl containing noodles, pour boiling water and let it stand as it is for about five minutes before draining the water and setting it aside for later use.

Step 2

Fry garlic in hot oil until brown before adding noodles frying it for about one minute.

Step 3

Now add egg into it and break it up when it starts to get solid, and mix it well into the noodles.

Step 4

Now add soy sauce, tofu, cilantro, bean sprouts, sugar and peanuts into it and mix it well.

Step 5

Remove from heat and add lime wedges just before you serve. Classical Pad Thai Noodles II

HUMMUS THAI STYLE

Prep Time: 15 mins - **Total Time:** 30 mins

SERVINGS: 12

NUTRITIONAL VALUE

Calories 142 kcal, Carbohydrates 13.8 g, Cholesterol 0 mg, Fat 9.4 g, Fiber 2.4 g, Protein 3.9 g, Sodium 315 mg

INGREDIENTS

- 1/4 cup coconut oil
- 1 jalapeno pepper, minced
- 2 large cloves garlic, very thinly sliced
- 1/2 tsp salt
- 2 cups cooked garbanzo beans
- 1 pinch cayenne pepper(optional)
- 1/4 cup fresh lime juice
- 1 pinch chili powder (optional)
- 1/4 cup peanut butter
- 1/4 cup coconut milk
- 1/4 cup sweet chili sauce
- 1/4 cup minced lemon grass

- 1/4 cup minced fresh Thai basil leaves
- 1 tbsp grated fresh ginger
- 2 tsps green curry paste

DIRECTIONS

Step 1

Cook garlic in hot coconut oil for about one minute and transfer it to a bowl.

Step 2

Put cooled garlic mixture, lime juice, coconut milk, chili sauce, lemon grass, basil, ginger, curry paste, garbanzo beans, jalapeno pepper, salt, peanut butter, cayenne pepper and chili in a blender and blend it until you find that it is smooth.

Step 3

Serve.

CURRY THAICHICKEN WITH PINEAPPLE

Prep Time: 15 mins - **Total Time:** 50 mins

SERVINGS: 6

NUTRITIONAL VALUE

Calories 623 kcal, Carbohydrates 77.5 g, Cholesterol 20 mg, Fat 34.5 g, Fiber 3.5 g, Protein 20.3 g, Sodium 781 mg

INGREDIENTS

- 2 cups uncooked jasmine rice
- 1 1/2 cups sliced bamboo shoots, drained
- 1 quart water
- 1/2 red bell pepper, julienned

- 1/4 cup red curry paste
- 1/2 green bell pepper, julienned
- 2 (13.5 ounce) cans coconut milk
- 1/2 small onion, chopped
- 2 skinless, boneless chicken breast halves
- 1 cup pineapple chunks, drained
- - cut into thin strips
- 3 tbsps fish sauce
- 1/4 cup white sugar

DIRECTIONS

Step 1

Bring the mixture of rice and water to boil before turning the heat down to low and cooking for 25 minutes.

Step 2

Add coconut milk, bamboo shoots, chicken, sugar and fish sauce to the mixture of curry paste and 1 can coconut milk in a pan before bringing all this to boil and cooking for 15 minutes.

Step 3

Into this mixture, add red bell pepper, onion and green bell pepper, and cook all this for ten more minutes or until you see that the peppers are tender.

Step 4

Add pineapple after removing from heat and serve this on top of cooked rice.

HOW TO MAKE PEANUT SAUCE

Prep Time: 10 mins - **Total Time:** 10 mins

SERVINGS: 6

NUTRITIONAL VALUE

Calories 130 kcal, Carbohydrates 9.8 g, Cholesterol 3 mg, Fat 9.5 g, Fiber 0.6 g, Protein 2.7 g, Sodium 529 mg

INGREDIENTS

- 1/4 cup creamy peanut butter
- 3 cloves garlic, minced
- 1/4 cup brown sugar
- 1/4 cup mayonnaise
- 1/4 cup soy sauce
- 2 tbsps fresh lemon juice

DIRECTIONS

Step 1

- Whisk all the ingredients that are mentioned above in a medium sized bowl and refrigerate it for at least two hours before you serve it to anyone.

BROWN RICE VEGETABLE SOUP

Prep Time: 15 mins - **Total Time:** 1 hr 30 mins

SERVINGS: 12

NUTRITIONAL VALUE

Calories 183 kcal, Carbohydrates 21.4 g, Cholesterol < 1 mg, Fat 7.4 g, Fiber 3 g, Protein 4.4 g, Sodium 749 mg

INGREDIENTS

- 1 cup uncooked brown rice
- 1 cup white wine
- 2 cups water

- 3 tbsps fish sauce
- 3 tbsps olive oil
- 2 tbsps soy sauce
- 1 sweet onion, chopped
- 3 Thai chili peppers
- 4 cloves garlic, minced
- 2 tbsps chopped fresh lemon grass
- 1/4 cup chopped fresh ginger root
- 1 tbsp Thai pepper garlic sauce
- 1 cup chopped carrots
- 1 tsp saffron
- 4 cups chopped broccoli
- 3/4 cup plain yogurt
- 1 red bell pepper, diced
- fresh cilantro, for garnish
- 1 (14 ounce) can light coconut milk
- 6 cups vegetable broth

DIRECTIONS

Step 1

- Bring the mixture of rice and water to boil before turning the heat down to low and cooking for 45 minutes.

Step 2

Cook ginger, carrots, garlic and onion in hot olive oil for about five minutes before you add broccoli, coconut milk, broth, wine, soy sauce, Thai chili peppers, red bell pepper, lemon grass, fish sauce, garlic sauce, and saffron into it and cook for another 25 minutes.

Step 3

Now blend this soup in batches in a blender until you get the required smoothness.

Step 4

Mix yoghurt and cooked rice very thoroughly with this soup.

Step 5

Garnish with cilantro before you serve.

THAI **ORANGE CHICKEN**

Prep Time: 15 mins - **Total Time:** 40 mins

SERVINGS: 12

NUTRITIONAL VALUE

Calories 427 kcal, Carbohydrates 37.1 g, Cholesterol 32 mg, Fat 24.3 g, Fiber 3.5 g, Protein 18.4 g, Sodium 1360 mg

INGREDIENTS

- 2 tbsps olive oil
- 1/3 cup soy sauce
- 3 carrots, cut into matchsticks
- 1/3 cup brown sugar
- 1/2 tsp minced fresh ginger root
- 2 tbsps ketchup
- 1 clove garlic, minced
- 1 tsp crushed red pepper flakes

- 2 tbsps olive oil
- 2 tbsps cornstarch
- 2 skinless, boneless chicken breast
- halves, cut into small pieces
- 1/2 cup water
- 1/2 cup peanuts
- 1/3 cup orange juice

DIRECTIONS

Step 1

Cook carrots, garlic and ginger in hot olive oil for about 5 minutes before transferring it to a bowl.

Step 2

Cook chicken in hot olive oil for about 10 minutes before adding carrot mixture, water, brown sugar , orange juice, soy sauce, peanuts, ketchup, and red pepper flakes into this, and cooking for another 5 minutes.

Step 3

Take out ¼ cup of sauce from the pan and add cornstarch into it.

Step 4

Add this cornstarch mixture back to the chicken and cook until you see that the required thickness has been reached.

JAPANESE BAKED SWEET POTATO

Prep Time: 10 mins - **Total Time:** 1 hr 10 mins

SERVINGS: 4

NUTRITIONAL VALUE

Calories 147.2, Fat 5.1g , Cholesterol 0.0mg , Sodium 535.3mg , Carbohydrates 23.3g , Protein 2.5g

INGREDIENTS

- 2 tbsp brown sugar
- 3 tbsp low soy sauce
- 2 tbsp mirin
- 1 tbsp dark sesame oil
- 4 garlic cloves, minced
- 2 -3 sweet potatoes, diced
- 1 tbsp toasted sesame seeds
- 1 sheet of toasted nori

DIRECTIONS

Step 1

Before you do anything preheat the oven to 400 F. Grease a casserole dish.

Step 2

Get a mixing bowl: Mix in it all the ingredients except for the potato to make the sauce.

Step 3

Lay potato slices over the casserole dish and drizzle the sauce all over it. Put on the lid then cook it in the oven for 52 min.

Step 4

Drizzle the dripping and the marinade from the casserole dish all over the potato. Remove the cover and cook it in the oven for 12 min.

Step 5

Top your baked potato with sesame seeds and nori. Serve it warm.

Step 6

Enjoy.

JAPANESE LUNCH BOX (MIRIN EGGPLANTS SALAD)

Prep Time: 10 mins - **Total Time:** 30 mins

SERVINGS: 4

NUTRITIONAL VALUE

Calories 368.3, Fat 12.3g , Cholesterol 0.0mg , Sodium 971.9mg , Carbohydrates 64.0g , Protein 12.7g

INGREDIENTS

- 8 Japanese eggplants
- 3 tbsp vegetable oil
- 1/4 tsp chili pepper flakes, to taste
- 1 packet dried bonito flakes
- 3 1/2 tbsp soy sauce
- 3 tbsp mirin
- 1 C. water

DIRECTIONS

Step 1

Score the eggplants with a sharp knife lengthwise after each half inch.

Step 2

Transfer the eggplant with the rest of the ingredients to a heavy saucepan. Cook them until they start simmering.

Step 3

Keep simmering the eggplant mix for 22 min while stirring it from time to time. Serve your eggplant salad.

Step 4

Enjoy.

JAPANESE **GREEN BEANS SALAD**

Prep Time: 5 mins - **Total Time:** 15 mins

SERVINGS: 4

NUTRITIONAL VALUE

Calories 109.9, Fat 3.6g , Cholesterol 0.0mg , Sodium 801.1mg , Carbohydrates 17.3g , Protein 4.9g

INGREDIENTS

- 500 g fresh green beans
- 3 tbsp sesame seeds
- 3 tbsp soy sauce
- 2 tbsp yellow sugar
- 1 pinch salt

DIRECTIONS

Step 1

Place a pan over medium heat. Toast the sesame seeds in it for 2 min. Transfer it to a pestle and grind it slightly.

Step 2

Get a large mixing bowl: Stir in it the sesame seeds with the soy sauce, sugar, and a pinch of salt. Whisk them well to make the dressing.

Step 3

Trim the green beans. Bring salted saucepan of water to a boil. Cook in it the green beans until they become light green.

Step 4

Remove them from the water and rinse them with some water to lose heat. Drain the and pat them dry.

Step 5

Toss the green beans with the dressing. Serve it.

Step 6

Enjoy.

JAPANESE SHRIMP STEW

Prep Time: 10 mins - **Total Time:** 35 mins

SERVINGS: 2

NUTRITIONAL VALUE

Calories 540.0, Fat 9.9g, Cholesterol 85.1mg, Sodium 1688.5mg, Carbohydrates 87.8g, Protein 22.0g

INGREDIENTS

- 2 1/2 C. dashi stock
- 3 tbsp soy sauce
- 2 tbsp mirin
- 1/2 tsp sesame oil
- 1 tbsp canola oil
- 2 spring onions, finely sliced
- 2 tsp finely grated ginger
- 1 C. japanese short-grain rice, uncooked

- 1/2 red pepper
- 12 snow peas, halved on the diagonal
- 16 large shrimp, uncooked

DIRECTIONS

Step 1

Get a small mixing bowl: Whisk in it the stock, soy sauce, mirin and sesame oil.

Step 2

Place a saucepan over medium heat. Heat the oil in it. Cook in it the green onion for 2 min.

Step 3

Stir in the rice with ginger. Cook them for 2 min. Stir in the stock and sauce mix, red pepper and snow peas. Cook the stew until it starts boiling.

Step 4

Put on the cover and lower the heat. Cook the stew for 17 min. Remove the lid and lay the shrimp on top.

Step 5

Put the lid back on and cook the stew for 6 min. Serve your stew warm.

Step 6

Enjoy.

JAPANESE **CHICKEN W/ BBQ BEANS AND SLAW**

Prep Time: 15 mins **- Total Time:** 1 hr 15 mins

SERVINGS: 4

NUTRITIONAL VALUE

Calories 746.4, Fat 20.5g , Cholesterol 118.2mg , Sodium 1063.7mg , Carbohydrates 109.2g , Protein 37.0g

INGREDIENTS

- 8 chicken drumsticks or 1 1/2-2 lbs
- chicken drumsticks
- 2 C. canned black-eyed peas, drained and
- 1 tbsp olive oil
- rinsed
- 1/4 C. ponzu sauce, lime sauce
- cooking spray
- 1 tbsp ketchup
- 1/2 head cabbage, cored
- 1/2 C. honey
- 1 medium carrot
- 1/2-1 garlic clove, minced
- 1 tbsp olive oil
- salt and pepper
- 2 tbsp rice vinegar
- 3/4 C. ketchup
- 1/2 C. pure maple syrup
- 2 tbsp pure maple syrup
- 1/2 tbsp liquid smoke flavoring
- 1 tbsp sriracha sauce
- 1/2 tsp dry mustard

- 1 tbsp lime juice
- 1/4 tsp garlic powder
- 1/2 tsp ground ginger
- salt and pepper
- salt
- 1 C. onion, chopped

DIRECTIONS

Step 1

To make the chicken drumsticks:

Step 2

Before you do anything preheat the oven to 375 F. Lay the chicken drumsticks in a greased casserole dish.

Step 3

Get a small mixing bowl: Whisk in it the soy sauce, ketchup, honey, garlic, salt and pepper.

Drizzle the mix all over the chicken drumsticks.

Step 4

Place the chicken pan in the oven and cook it for 30 min. Flip the chicken drumsticks and cook them for another 30 min.

Step 5

To make the barbecued beans:

Step 6

Place a heavy saucepan over medium heat: Stir in it the ketchup, pure maple syrup, smoke flavoring, mustard powder, garlic powder, salt and pepper. Cook them for 10 min.

Step 7

In the meantime, chop the onion and cook it in a greased pan for 6 min. Transfer the cooked onion with black eyed peas into the saucepan.

Step 8

Put on the lid and coo them until the bean becomes thick. Japanese Chicken w/ BBQ Beans and Slaw

Step 9

Cut the carrot and cabbage into thin strips.

Step 10

To make the hot slaw:

Step 11

Grease a wok or a pan with a cooking spray. Cook in it the carrot and cabbage for 4 min.

Step 12

Get a small bowl: Whisk in it the olive oil, rice vinegar, pure maple syrup, Sriracha Hot Chili sauce, lime juice, ground ginger, salt and pepper to make the dressing.

Step 13

Drizzle the sauce all over the carrot and cabbage mix. Cook them for 3 min.

Step 14

Serve your chicken drumsticks warm with the barbecued beans and warm hot slaw.

Step 15

Enjoy.

JAPANESE **CHICKEN SOUP**

Prep Time: 10 mins **- Total Time:** 15 mins

SERVINGS: 4

NUTRITIONAL VALUE

Calories 210.7, Fat 5.7g , Cholesterol 125.9mg , Sodium 733.6mg , Carbohydrates 6.3g , Protein 28.0g

INGREDIENTS

- 1 lb ground chicken or 1 lb pork
- 1/4 C. miso
- 1/4 C. sake
- 1/4 C. fresh ginger, grated
- 1 egg
- flour or starch, as needed
- green onion, chopped

DIRECTIONS

Step 1

Get a small bowl: Whisk in it the miso with sake.

Step 2

Get a mixing bowl: Combine in it all the ingredients. Mix them well.

Step 3

Bring some nabe broth to a boil in a large saucepan. Drop the chicken mix using a tbsp into the hot broth and cook them until they are no longer pink.

Step 4

Serve your chicken meatballs soup warm.

Step 5

Enjoy.

OKONOMIYAKI **JAPANESE PANCAKES**

Prep Time: 15 mins - **Total Time:** 45 mins

SERVINGS: 4

NUTRITIONAL VALUE

Calories 659 kcal, Carbohydrates 90.7 g, Cholesterol 217 mg, Fat 19.4 g, Fiber 8.3 g, Protein 29.3 g, Sodium 1531 mg

INGREDIENTS

- 12 ounces sliced bacon
- 1 1/3 cups water
- 4 eggs
- 3 cups all-purpose flour
- 1 tsp salt
- 1 medium head cabbage, cored and sliced
- 2 tbsps minced pickled ginger
- 1/4 cup tonkatsu sauce or barbeque sauce

DIRECTIONS

Step 1

Get a frying pan. Bacon should be fried with a medium heat. Soak excess oils with paper towel and put to the side.

Step 2

Get a bowl. Combine some water and eggs. Next combine in slowly, your flour, and then add salt.

Step 3

Combine with the flour: the ginger, and cabbage and mix until even.

Step 4

Get a 2nd frying pan or use the one from earlier. Add some nonstick spray to it. Take 1 / 4 cup of batter and put it in the middle of the pan.

Step 5

Cover the batter with 4 bacon strips. Make sure the batter is circular. Fry for 6 mins. Turn over the batter and cook the opposite side until golden. Set aside.

Step 6

Garnish with tonkatsu sauce. Cook all the batter in the same manner.

Step 7

Enjoy.

CUCUMBER SALAD IN JAPAN

Prep Time: 15 mins - **Total Time:** 45 mins

SERVINGS: 4

NUTRITIONAL VALUE

Calories 55 kcal, Carbohydrates 10.5 g, Cholesterol 0 mg, Fat 1.6 g, Fiber 1 g, Protein 0.8 g, Sodium 111 mg

INGREDIENTS

- 2 tbsps white sugar
- 2 tbsps rice vinegar
- 1 tsp Asian (toasted) sesame oil
- 1 tsp chili pastc (sambal oelek)
- salt to taste
- 2 large cucumbers - peeled, seeded, and
- cut into 1/4-inch slices

DIRECTIONS

Step 1

Get a bowl. Mix the following evenly: salt, sugar, chili paste, sesame oil, and rice vinegar.

Step 2

Combine with the wet mixture, your cucumbers, and set the salad to marinade for 35 mins on a countertop.

Step 3

Enjoy the salad at room temp.

CHICKEN WINGS IN JAPAN

Prep Time: 15 mins - **Total Time:** 1 hr

SERVINGS: 6

NUTRITIONAL VALUE

Calories 675 kcal, Carbohydrates 51.4 g, Cholesterol 158 mg, Fat 44.3 g, Fiber 0.7 g, Protein 18.9 g, Sodium 1112 mg

INGREDIENTS

- 3 pounds chicken wings
- 1 egg, lightly beaten
- 1 cup all-purpose flour for coating
- 1 cup butter
- SAUCE
- 3 tbsps soy sauce
- 3 tbsps water
- 1 cup white sugar
- 1/2 cup white vinegar
- 1/2 tsp garlic powder, or to taste
- 1 tsp salt

DIRECTIONS

Step 1

Get your oven to 350 degrees before doing anything else.

Step 2

Slice your wings into two pieces. Get two bowls: one with egg, another with flour.

Step 3

Coat the wings with egg first, then flour.

Step 4

Get a frying pan and get butter melted.

Step 5

Fry wings until completely golden brown.

Step 6

Then move the wings into a saucepan.

Step 7

Get a bowl mix the following: salt, soy sauce, garlic powder, water, vinegar, and sugar. Use to coat wings.

Step 8

Enter wings into the oven for 40 mins. Make sure to baste with remaining wet mixture occasionally.

Step 9

Enjoy.

JAPANESE **ZUCCHINI STIR FRY**

Prep Time: 10 mins - **Total Time:** 20 mins

SERVINGS: 4

NUTRITIONAL VALUE

Calories 110 kcal, Carbohydrates 8.1 g, Cholesterol 0 mg, Fat 8.2 g, Fiber 1.9 g, Protein 2.7 g, Sodium 581 mg

INGREDIENTS

- 2 tbsps vegetable oil
- 1 medium onion, thinly sliced
- 2 medium zucchinis, cut into thin strips
- 2 tbsps teriyaki sauce
- 1 tbsp soy sauce
- 1 tbsp toasted sesame seeds
- ground black pepper

DIRECTIONS

Step 1

Get a frying pan hot with oil. For 5 mins stir fry onions.

Step 2

Add and stir-fry zucchini for an additional min.

Step 3

Combine into the zucchini your sesame seeds, teriyaki sauce, and soy sauce. Fry for 5 mins.

Step 4

Finally add pepper.

Step 5

Enjoy.

JAPANESE FRUIT PIE

Prep Time: 10 mins - **Total Time:** 1 hr

SERVINGS: 1 pie

NUTRITIONAL VALUE

Calories 404 kcal, Carbohydrates 47.7 g, Cholesterol 67 mg, Fat 23.1 g, Fiber 1.7 g, Protein 3.8 g, Sodium 243 mg

INGREDIENTS

- 1 (9 inch) unbaked pie shell
- 2 eggs, beaten
- 1/3 cup butter, melted
- 1 cup white sugar
- 1 tsp vanilla extract
- 1 tbsp distilled white vinegar
- 1/2 cup chopped pecans
- 1/2 cup shredded coconut
- 1/2 cup raisins

DIRECTIONS

Step 1

Get your oven hot to 350 degrees.

Step 2

Get a bowl. Mix together until even and smooth: vinegar, eggs, sugar and butter.

Step 3

Mix in raisins, pecans, and coconut. Put everything in a pie crust.

Step 4

Bake for 40 mins.

Step 5

Enjoy.

JAPANESE **BEEF STIR-FRY**

Prep Time: 30 mins - **Total Time:** 45 mins

SERVINGS: 8

NUTRITIONAL VALUE

Calories 290 kcal, Carbohydrates 26.4 g, Cholesterol 39 mg, Fat 7.6 g, Fiber 2.6 g, Protein 26.4 g, Sodium 1271 mg

INGREDIENTS

- 2 pounds boneless beef sirloin or beef top
- round steaks (3/4" thick)
- sliced
- 3 tbsps cornstarch
- 2 medium red peppers, cut into 2"-long strips 1 (10.5 ounce) can Campbell's® Condensed
- 3 stalks celery, sliced
- Beef Broth
- 2 medium green onions, cut into 2" pieces 1/2 cup soy sauce
- Hot cooked regular long-grain white rice
- 2 tbsps sugar
- 2 tbsps vegetable oil
- 4 cups sliced shiitake mushrooms
- 1 head Chinese cabbage (bok choy), thinly

DIRECTIONS

Step 1

To start this recipe grab a knife and begin to cut your beef into some thin long strips.

Step 2

Grab a medium sized bowl and combine the following ingredients: sugar, broth, soy, and cornstarch.

Step 3

After combining the ingredients set them aside.

Step 4

Get your wok hot over a high level of heat and add one 1 tbsp of oil to it.

Step 5

Once your oil is hot combine the following ingredients in it: green onions, mushrooms, celery, cabbage, and peppers.

Step 6

Fry these veggies down until you find that they are soft. Set aside.

Step 7

Now grab your cornstarch mixture and put it in the pot. Stir-fry until you find that it has thickened.

Step 8

Once thick, combine the cornstarch with your beef and veggies.

Step 9

Fry until beef is cooked completely.

Step 10

Let contents cool.

Step 11

Enjoy.

JAPANESE TOFU MUSHROOM SOUP

Prep Time: 10 mins - **Total Time:** 20 mins

SERVINGS: 2 servings

NUTRITIONAL VALUE

Calories 100 kcal, Carbohydrates 4.8 g, Cholesterol 3 mg, Fat 3.9 g, Fiber 1 g, Protein 11 g, Sodium 1326 mg

INGREDIENTS

- 3 cups prepared dashi stock
- 1/4 cup sliced shiitake mushrooms
- 1 tbsp miso paste
- 1 tbsp soy sauce
- 1/8 cup cubed soft tofu
- 1 green onion, diced

DIRECTIONS

Step 1

Get a saucepan. Add your stock, get it boiling. Once boiling add mushrooms and cook for 4 mins.

Step 2

Get a bowl. Combine soy sauce and miso paste evenly. Mix this with your stock.

Step 3

For 6 mins let broth cook. Add some diced green onion.

Step 4

Enjoy.

JAPANESE **UDON SOUP**

Prep Time: 15 mins - **Total Time:** 40 mins

SERVINGS: 4

NUTRITIONAL VALUE

Calories 548 kcal, Carbohydrates 53.4 g, Cholesterol 206 mg, Fat 17.2 g, Fiber 2.8 g, Protein 42.2 g, Sodium 2491 mg

INGREDIENTS

- 6 cups prepared dashi stock
- 1/4 pound chicken, cut into chunks
- 1 (9 ounce) package fresh udon noodles
- 2 carrots, diced
- 4 eggs
- 1/3 cup soy sauce
- 2 leeks, diced
- 3 tbsps mirin
- 1/2 tsp white sugar
- 1/3 tsp salt
- 2 (12 ounce) packages firm tofu, cubed
- 1/3 pound shiitake mushrooms, sliced
- 5 ribs and leaves of bok choy, diced

DIRECTIONS

Step 1

Get a sauce pan. Heat the following: salt, dashi stock, sugar, carrots, mirin, chicken, and soy sauce. Allow everything to lightly boil until your chicken is cooked fully (8 mins).

Step 2

Mix in some bok choy, mushrooms, and tofu. Let everything continue simmering for 6 mins.

Step 3

Add your noodles and cook for 5 more mins. Finally add leeks.

Step 4

Take your eggs and crack them over the soup. Let the soup cook for 5 mins until eggs are done.

Step 5

Enjoy.

DEVILED EGGS JAPANESE II

Prep Time: 35 mins - **Total Time:** 55 mins

SERVINGS: 18

NUTRITIONAL VALUE

Calories 91 kcal, Carbohydrates 2.1 g, Cholesterol 95 mg, Fat 7.9 g, Fiber 0.1 g, Protein 3.6 g, Sodium 122 mg

INGREDIENTS

- 9 eggs
- 2 tbsps sesame seeds
- 1/2 cup mayonnaise
- 2 tsps soy sauce
- 2 tsps wasabi paste
- 2 tsps rice wine vinegar
- 2 tbsps thinly sliced green onions

- 4 tbsps panko bread crumbs

DIRECTIONS

Step 1

Boil your eggs in a saucepan. Once the water is boiling let it continue about 10 to 15 mins.

Drain the water and run cold water over your eggs.

Step 2

Remove the shells. Place the eggs to the side.

Step 3

Get a frying pan and fry some sesame seeds for 4 mins. Set seeds aside.

Step 4

Split your shelled eggs and remove the yolks.

Step 5

Get your food processor and process the following until smooth: egg yolks, rice vinegar, mayo, wasabi paste and soy sauce.

Step 6

Put in some bread crumbs and green onion and pulse it a few more times.

Step 7

Put the processed contents into the center of your eggs and garnish each egg with sesame seeds.

Step 8

Enjoy.

JAPANESE SALAD DRESSING II

Prep Time: 15 mins - **Total Time:** 15 mins

SERVINGS: 1.25 cups

NUTRITIONAL VALUE

Calories 220 kcal, Carbohydrates 6.3 g, Cholesterol 0 mg, Fat 21.9 g, Fiber 0.5 g, Protein 0.9 g, Sodium 464 mg

INGREDIENTS

- 2 tbsps minced fresh ginger root
- 1/3 cup minced onion
- 1/4 cup minced celery
- 1/4 cup low-sodium soy sauce
- 1/2 lime, juiced
- 1 tbsp white sugar
- 1 tbsp ketchup
- 1/4 tsp ground black pepper
- 1/2 cup vegetable oil

DIRECTIONS

Step 1

Get a food processor. Process the following: celery, onion, and ginger until smooth.

Step 2

Mix in the following with your celery: pepper, soy sauce, ketchup, sugar and lime juice.

Process for 30 secs until smooth.

Step 3

Continually run the processor while adding oil until everything becomes dressing-like.

Step 4

Enjoy.

JAPANESE RICE AND EGGS

Prep Time: 5 mins - **Total Time:** 20 mins

SERVINGS: 1

NUTRITIONAL VALUE

Calories 521 kcal, Carbohydrates 59.3 g, Cholesterol 403 mg, Fat 20.2 g, Fiber 0.8 g, Protein 26.7 g, Sodium 1300 mg

INGREDIENTS

- 1 cup cooked white or brown rice
- 2 thin slices cooked ham, cubed
- 2 tbsps ketchup
- 1 slice processed cheese food (such as
- Velveeta ®) (optional)
- 2 eggs
- salt and pepper to taste
- 1 tbsp ketchup
- 1/4 tsp chopped fresh parsley

DIRECTIONS

Step 1

Get a frying pan, add nonstick spray. Combine your ham, cheese, 2 tbsps of ketchup, and cooked rice in the pan. Fry for about 9 mins.

Step 2

Put everything in a bowl or container.

Step 3

Get another bowl and whisk pepper, salt and eggs together.

Step 4

Get another frying pan and use some nonstick spray. Pour in eggs. As the edge of the egg cooks you should lift it. So the uncooked portion runs underneath. Do this until everything is fully cooked. Turn off the stove.

Step 5

Fold egg into a semi-circle and place on top of the rice.

Step 6

You can also add a tbsp of ketchup and parsley for a garnish.

Step 7

Enjoy.

JAPANESE **MACKEREL**

Prep Time: 20 mins **- Total Time:** 30 mins

SERVINGS: 4

NUTRITIONAL VALUE

Calories 234 kcal, Carbohydrates 9.2 g, Cholesterol 53 mg, Fat 9 g, Fiber 0.1 g, Protein 23.9 g,Sodium 1000 mg

INGREDIENTS

- 4 mackerel fillets
- 1/4 cup soy sauce
- 1/4 cup mirin (Japanese sweet wine)
- 1 tbsp white sugar
- 1/2 tbsp grated fresh ginger root

DIRECTIONS

Step 1

Clean your fish with cold water and remove any excess water with paper towels.

Step 2

Get a bowl and combine the following evenly: ginger, soy sauce, sugar, and mirin. Use as a marinade for your fish. Place a lid on the bowl. Chill contents for 25 mins.

Step 3

Turn on your broiler and get it hot, a grill could be used also.

Step 4

Place fillets under the broiler for 9 mins. Try to baste the fish a few times throughout the cooking time.

Step 5

Drizzle with lemon juice or radish.

Step 6

Enjoy.

JAPANESE **MUSHROOMS**

Prep Time: 5 mins **- Total Time:** 15 mins

SERVINGS: 2

NUTRITIONAL VALUE

Calories 196 kcal, Carbohydrates 14.2 g, Cholesterol 0 mg, Fat 14.1 g, Fiber 3.6 g, Protein 7.3 g, Sodium 1367 mg

INGREDIENTS

- 4 Portobello mushroom caps
- 3 tbsps soy sauce
- 2 tbsps sesame oil
- 1 tbsp minced fresh ginger root

- 1 small clove garlic, minced

DIRECTIONS

Step 1

Set your broiler to low. The rack should be placed 6 inches from the heating source (ideally).

Step 2

Run mushrooms under cold water until clean. Place mushrooms with the top's down on the baking sheet.

Step 3

Get a bowl mix the following evenly: sesame oil, garlic, soy sauce, and ginger. Cover the tops of the mushrooms with it.

Step 4

Cook mushrooms for 10 mins.

Step 5

Enjoy.

JAPANESE TOFU BURGER

Prep Time: 25 mins - **Total Time:** 45 mins

SERVINGS: 6

NUTRITIONAL VALUE

Calories 307 kcal, Carbohydrates 8.9 g, Cholesterol 77 mg, Fat 18.1 g, Fiber 2.1 g, Protein 25.5 g, Sodium 999 mg

INGREDIENTS

- 1 (14 ounce) package firm tofu
- 1/4 tsp minced fresh ginger root
- 1 pound ground beef

- 1 tbsp vegetable oil
- 1/2 cup sliced shiitake mushrooms
- 2 tbsps miso paste
- 1 egg, lightly beaten
- 1 tsp salt
- 1 tsp ground black pepper
- 1/4 tsp ground nutmeg
- 1/4 cup mirin (Japanese sweet wine)
- 2 tbsps soy sauce
- 1 tsp garlic paste

DIRECTIONS

Step 1

Remove excess liquid from your tofu. By placing it between two plates for 20 mins. Using something heavy on top to apply a constant downward force.

Step 2

Dice tofu into cubes.

Step 3

Get a bowl and mix the following: nutmeg, tofu, pepper, shiitake, salt, miso paste, and egg.

Form 6 balls from this mixture and shape them into burgers.

Step 4

Get another bowl and mix the following: ginger, mirin, garlic paste, and soy sauce. Put to the side.

Step 5

Get a frying pan. Heat veggie oil.

Step 6

Fry burgers for 2 mins each side. Set heat to low. Place a lid on the pan.

Step 7

Let the burgers lightly fry for 5 mins.

Step 8

Remove excess oils. Then cover the burgers with the wet mixture of soy sauce. Coat both sides of the burgers by turning them over.

Step 9

Enjoy.

JAPANESE SHRIMP SAUCE

Prep Time: 5 mins **- Total Time:** 5 mins

SERVINGS: 2.5 cups

NUTRITIONAL VALUE

Calories 161 kcal, Carbohydrates 1.3 g, Cholesterol 8 mg, Fat 17.5 g, Fiber 0.1 g, Protein 0.3 g, Sodium 172 mg

INGREDIENTS

- 2 cups mayonnaise
- 1/2 cup water
- 1 tsp white sugar
- 1 tsp paprika
- 1 tsp garlic juice
- 1 tbsp ketchup
- 1 tsp ground ginger
- 1 tsp hot pepper sauce

- 1 tsp ground mustard
- 1/4 tsp salt
- 3/4 tsp ground white pepper

DIRECTIONS

Step 1

Get a bowl and combine all the ingredients.

Step 2

Serve at room temperature. But store chilled.

Step 3

Enjoy.

JAPANESE **ONION SOUP**

Prep Time: 15 mins **- Total Time:** 1 hr

SERVINGS: 6

NUTRITIONAL VALUE

Calories 25 kcal, Carbohydrates 4.4 g, Cholesterol 1 mg, Fat 0.2 g, Fiber 0.9 g, Protein 1.4 g, Sodium 257 mg

INGREDIENTS

- 1/2 stalk celery, diced
- 1 small onion, diced
- 2 quarts water
- 1/2 carrot, diced
- 1 cup baby Portobello mushrooms, sliced
- 1 tsp grated fresh ginger root

- 1 tbsp minced fresh chives
- 1/4 tsp minced fresh garlic
- 2 tbsps chicken stock
- 3 tsps beef bouillon granules
- 1 cup chopped fresh shiitake mushrooms

DIRECTIONS

Step 1

Get a saucepan with high heat. Get the following items boiling before continuing: water, celery, beef bouillon, onion, chicken stock, carrots, half of the mushrooms, ginger, and garlic.

Step 2

Put a lid on the boiling contents. Set heat to a medium level. Let the contents lightly boil for 45 mins.

Step 3

Get another saucepan. Put the other half of mushrooms in it. Once the first pot has been cooking for 45 mins. Strain soup into the pot with uncooked mushrooms.

Step 4

Throw away anything left from the straining.

Step 5

Garnish with chives when served.

Step 6

Enjoy.

OSAKA BEEF ROLLS

Prep Time: 30 mins - **Total Time:** 40 mins

SERVINGS: 8

NUTRITIONAL VALUE

Calories 689 kcal, Carbohydrates 5.9 g, Cholesterol 242 mg, Fat 29.1 g, Fiber 2.1 g, Protein 95.1 g, Sodium 583 mg

INGREDIENTS

- 1 tbsp vegetable oil
- 12 shiitake mushrooms, sliced
- 24 spears fresh asparagus, trimmed
- 8 thin-cut top round steaks
- 1/4 cup soy sauce
- 1 bunch green onions, green parts only

DIRECTIONS

Step 1

Get a frying pan hot with oil. Place mushrooms in the pan. Put a lid on the pan. Set the heat to low. Cook until the mushrooms are soft, but not browned.

Step 2

Boil some water in a second pot and fill a bowl with ice and water. Once the water is boiling. Dip your asparagus in the boiling water and then enter the asparagus into the ice water. Put to the side. (Do this for all spears.)

Step 3

Heat your broiler. Apply some oil or nonstick spray to a broiler pan.

Step 4

Flatten steaks to 1/4 of an inch. Coat them with soy sauce then layer the following: 3

asparagus pieces, some mushrooms, and some green onions.

Step 5

Shape the steak into a roll-up. The seam portion of the steak should be placed at the bottom. Put a toothpick through each roll.

Step 6

Broil the steak for 4 mins. Then turn them. Broil for 3 mins.

Step 7

Be careful not to burn them.

Step 8

Enjoy.

JAPANESE **BEEF CROQUETTES**

Prep Time: 10 mins - **Total Time:** 30 mins

SERVINGS: 10

NUTRITIONAL VALUE

Calories 239 kcal, Carbohydrates 20.4 g, Cholesterol 69 mg, Fat 3.9 g, Fiber 1.5 g, Protein 9.6 g, Sodium 196 mg

INGREDIENTS

- 3 medium russet potatoes, peeled, and chopped
- 2 eggs, beaten
- 1 tbsp butterpanko bread crumbs
- 1 tbsp vegetable oil
- 1/2 cup oil for frying
- 3 onions, diced
- 3/4 pound ground beef
- 4 tsps light soy sauce
- all-purpose flour for coating

DIRECTIONS

Step 1

Get a saucepan. Boil salted water and potatoes for 16 mins. Remove water and put potatoes in a separate bowl. Combine some butter with the potatoes and mash them.

Step 2

Get a frying pan. Heat 1 tbsp of oil. Stir fry onions until soft. Add your soy sauce and beef to the onions.

Step 3

Continue to stir fry beef until browned and no liquid remains.

Step 4

Mix beef with the potatoes evenly.

Step 5

Get another frying pan hot with half a cup of oil.

Step 6

Form your mashed potatoes and beef into 10 patties and coat them with flour, then eggs, then bread crumbs.

Step 7

Finally fry each patty until golden on all sides.

Step 8

Remove excess oil and enjoy.

KYOTO CABBAGE

Prep Time: 25 mins - **Total Time:** 25 mins

SERVINGS: 12

NUTRITIONAL VALUE

Calories 126 kcal, Carbohydrates 8.1 g, Cholesterol 0 mg, Fat 9.6 g, Fiber 3 g, Protein 3.5 g, Sodium 208 mg

INGREDIENTS

- 3 tbsps sesame oil
- 1/4 cup toasted sesame seeds
- 3 tbsps rice vinegar
- 1 clove garlic, minced (optional)
- 1 tsp grated fresh ginger root (optional)
- 1 tbsp white sugar (optional)
- 1 tsp salt
- 1 tsp black pepper
- 1/2 large head cabbage, cored and
- shredded
- 1 bunch green onions, thinly sliced
- 1 cup almond slivers

DIRECTIONS

Step 1

Combine all the ingredients in a large bowl. Mix the wet ingredient first, then the dry ones.

Toss everything so the cabbage is evenly coated.

Step 2

Enjoy at room temperature or chilled.

JAPANESE **FRIED CHICKEN**

Prep Time: 20 mins - **Total Time:** 1 hr 10 mins

SERVINGS: 8

NUTRITIONAL VALUE

Calories 256 kcal, Carbohydrates 4.8 g, Cholesterol 98 mg, Fat 16.7 g, Fiber 0.1 g, Protein 20.9 g, Sodium 327 mg

INGREDIENTS

- 2 eggs, lightly beaten
- 1/2 tsp salt
- breast halves - cut into 1 inch cubes
- 1/2 tsp black pepper
- 3 tbsps potato starch
- 1/2 tsp white sugar
- 1 tbsp rice flour
- 1 tbsp minced garlic
- oil for frying
- 1 tbsp grated fresh ginger root
- 1 tbsp sesame oil
- 1 tbsp soy sauce
- 1/8 tsp chicken bouillon granules
- 1 1/2 pounds skinless, boneless chicken

DIRECTIONS

Step 1

Get a bowl and combine the following: bouillon, eggs, soy sauce, salt, sesame oil, pepper, ginger, garlic, and sugar. Use as a marinade for the chicken. Place a lid over the contents.

And let the chicken marinate in this mixture at least 35 mins in the frig.

Step 2

Take off the lid from the marinade and add rice flour and potato starch to it. Evenly combine everything.

Step 3

Get a frying pan and get oil to 365 degrees.

Step 4

Fry your chicken until brown in a batch process.

Step 5

Remove excess oil.

Step 6

Enjoy.

EASY KATSU

Prep Time: 10 mins - **Total Time:** 20 mins

SERVINGS: 4

NUTRITIONAL VALUE

Calories 297 kcal, Carbohydrates 22.2 g, Cholesterol 118 mg, Fat 11.4 g, Fiber 0.1 g, Protein 31.2 g, Sodium 251 mg

INGREDIENTS

- 4 skinless, boneless chicken breast halves
- - pounded to 1/2 inch thickness
- salt and pepper to taste
- 2 tbsps all-purpose flour
- 1 egg, beaten
- 1 cup panko bread crumbs

- 1 cup oil for frying, or as needed

DIRECTIONS

Step 1

Get three bowls. Bowl 1 for chicken with some pepper and salt. Bowl 2 for bread crumbs.

Bowl 3 for eggs.

Step 2

Cover chicken with flour first. Then with egg, and finally with crumbs.

Step 3

Get a frying pan and heat 1/4 inch of oil. Fry your chicken for 5 mins on each side.

Step 4

Remove excess oil.

Step 5

Enjoy.

JAPANESE **SPINACH**

Prep Time: 5 mins **- Total Time:** 10 mins

SERVINGS: 6

NUTRITIONAL VALUE

Calories 101 kcal, Carbohydrates 6.7 g, Cholesterol 0 mg, Fat 7.9 g, Fiber 2.5 g, Protein 3.4 g, Sodium 66 mg

INGREDIENTS

- 2 tbsps sesame oil
- 1 tbsp brown sugar
- 10 cups fresh spinach leaves

- 4 tbsps black sesame seeds, toasted

DIRECTIONS

Step 1

Get a frying pan and get sesame oil hot. Combine spinach with oil in 3 cup batches. Fry until completely wilted. Then mix in another 3 cups of spinach.

Step 2

Smash your sesame seeds into small crumbs. Set to the side.

Step 3

Once your spinach is completely wilted create a hole in the center of the spinach. In the hole add sugar and cook until melted down. Mix spinach and sugar together completely.

Step 4

Serve with a garnish of crushed sesame seeds.

Step 5

Enjoy.

JAPANESE TOFU AND MISO

Prep Time: 15 mins - **Total Time:** 20 mins

SERVINGS: 6

NUTRITIONAL VALUE

Calories 82 kcal, Carbohydrates 4.6 g, Cholesterol 6 mg, Fat 4.5 g, Fiber 0.9 g, Protein 7.4 g, Sodium 358 mg

INGREDIENTS

- 2 tbsps sesame seeds
- 1/2 cup dried Asian-style whole sardines
- 2 1/2 tbsps red miso paste

- 1/2 cup boiling water
- 1 (16 ounce) package silken tofu, cubed
- 4 green onions, thinly sliced
- crushed red pepper flakes

DIRECTIONS

Step 1

Get a skillet and fry sesame seeds until aromatic for 3 mins.

Step 2

Get a pan and begin to boil water.

Step 3

Get a food processor and combine dried sardines and sesame seeds. Process into a powder.

Step 4

Put sesame and sardines in a bowl and combine miso. Combine in your boiling water (1/2 cup) from earlier and mix until creamy.

Step 5

Finally combine your tofu red pepper, and green onions.

Step 6

Enjoy.

HOW TO MAKE RAMEN SOUP SIMPLY

Prep Time: 5 mins - **Total Time:** 15 mins

SERVINGS: 2

NUTRITIONAL VALUE

Calories 291 kcal, Fat 10.2 g, Carbohydrates 42.4g, Protein 6.9 g, Cholesterol 0 mg, Sodium 1675 mg

INGREDIENTS

- 3 1/2 C. vegetable broth
- 1 (3.5 oz.) package ramen noodles with
- dried vegetables
- 2 tsp soy sauce
- 1/2 tsp chili oil
- 1/2 tsp minced fresh ginger root
- 2 green onions, sliced

DIRECTIONS

Step 1

In a medium pan, add the noodles and broth over high heat.

Step 2

Cover the pan and bring to a boil.

Step 3

Uncover the pan and stir to break up the noodles.

Step 4

Reduce the heat to medium and stir in the ginger, soy sauce and chili oil.

Step 5

Simmer, uncovered for about 10 minutes.

Step 6

Stir in the sesame oil and serve with a garnishing of the green onions.

FULL **RAMEN BREAKFAST**

Prep Time: 5 mins - **Total Time:** 35 mins

SERVINGS: 4

NUTRITIONAL VALUE

Calories 383 kcal, Fat 31.1 g, Carbohydrates 4.7g, Protein 20.7 g, Cholesterol 243 mg, Sodium 836 mg

DIRECTIONS

INGREDIENTS

Step 1

Set your oven to 350 degrees F before doing anything 8 slices turkey baconelse. 2 (3 oz.) packages ramen noodles,

Step 2

Heat a 12-inch oven proof nonstick skillet on medium break each block into 4 pieces heat and cook the bacon for about 8 minutes, stirring (flavor packets discarded)continuously. 1 1/2 tbsp vegetable oil, divided

Step 3

Transfer the bacon onto paper towels lined plate to drain. 1 C. shredded Cheddar cheese **Step 4**

Remove skillet from heat and discard the bacon grease, 1 tbsp butter 4 eggs leaving 1 tbsp in the skillet.

Step 5

In a pan of salted boiling water, cook the ramen noodles about 3 minutes, stirring occasionally.

Step 6

Drain the noodles in a colander and rinse under cold water.

Step 7

Heat the skillet of bacon grease on medium-high heat.

Step 8

In the bottom of skillet, place the noodles evenly and cook for about 3-6 minutes, pressing occasionally with a slotted spatula.

Step 9

Carefully, slide the ramen cake onto a large plate.

Step 10

Now, invert a second plate over top and flip cake over, cooked side upwards.

Step 11

In the same skillet, heat 1 tbsp of the oil on medium-high heat.

Step 12

Carefully, slide ramen cake into skillet and cook for about 3-5 minutes, pressing occasionally with a slotted spatula.

Step 13

Sprinkle with the cheese evenly and transfer the skillet into oven.

Step 14

Cook in the oven for about 5-10 minutes.

Step 15

Remove from the oven and transfer ramen cake onto a cutting board.

Step 16

Carefully, cut into 4 wedges.

Step 17

With the paper towels, wipe out the skillet.

Step 18

In the same skillet, heat remaining 1/2 tbsp of the oil and butter on medium heat.

Step 19

Carefully, crack eggs into skillet and cook for about 2-3 minutes.

Step 20

In each serving plate, place 1 ramen wedge, 1 fried egg and 2 bacon slices and serve.

KOREAN KIMCHEE SQUATS

Prep Time: 25 mins - **Total Time:** 1 day 5 hrs

SERVINGS: 8

NUTRITIONAL VALUE

Calories 36 kcal, Carbohydrates 6.8 g, Cholesterol 0 mg, Fat 0.5 g, Fiber 1.9 g, Protein 2.6 g, Sodium 1796 mg

INGREDIENTS

- 2 lbs. chopped Chinese cabbage
- 1 dash sesame oil
- 1 tbsp. salt
- 2 tbsps. chopped green onion
- 1 clove garlic, crushed
- 1 tbsp. chili powder
- 2 tsps. minced fresh ginger root
- half cup light soy sauce
- half cup white wine vinegar
- 2 tsps. white sugar

DIRECTIONS

Step 1

Let cabbage sit for 4 hours after adding some salt and massage it with your hands until you find that it is soft.

Step 2

Now drain all the liquid and add green onion, soy sauce, sugar, ginger, garlic and chili powder into this cabbage.

Step 3

Refrigerate for about 24 hours in a jar before serving.

KOREAN **SALAD W/ SESAME DRESSING**

Prep Time: 10 mins **- Total Time:** 10 mins

SERVINGS: 5

NUTRITIONAL VALUE

Calories 80 kcal, Carbohydrates 6.1 g, Cholesterol 0 mg, Fat 5.9 g, Fiber 1.6 g, Protein 2 g, Sodium 740 mg

INGREDIENTS

- 1 head red leaf lettuce
- 4 green onions (white part only)
- 1/4 cup soy sauce
- 5 tbsps. water
- 2 tsps. white sugar
- 1/4 cup distilled white vinegar
- 2 tbsps. sesame oil
- 1 tbsp. red pepper flakes

DIRECTIONS

Step 1

Place lettuce leaves into a bowl after washing and cutting.

Step 2

Now add the sliced white portion of your sliced green onions into the bowl containing the lettuce leaves.

Step 3

In a separate bowl mix soy sauce, white sugar, vinegar, sesame oil, water, and red pepper flakes and pour this mixture over the bowl containing lettuce leaves and green onions.

Step 4

Serve.

SPICY RED PEPPER CUCUMBERS

Prep Time: 10 mins - **Total Time:** 15 mins

SERVINGS: 2

NUTRITIONAL VALUE

Calories 1092 kcal, Carbohydrates 57.5 g, Cholesterol 155 mg, Fat 78.6 g, Fiber 1.8 g, Protein 39.1 g, Sodium 2501 mg

INGREDIENTS

- 1 tsp. vegetable oil
- 1 cucumber, halved, seeded and thinly sliced 2 tbsps. sesame seeds
- 2 tbsps. kochujang (Korean hot sauce)
- 1/4 cup white vinegar
- 1 tbsp. sesame oil
- 1 green onion, chopped

DIRECTIONS

Step 1

Place sesame seeds in a large bowl after cooking in hot vegetable oil for about three minutes and add kochujang, green onion and sesame oil into the sesame seeds.

Step 2

Now add cucumber and mix well.

Step 3

Serve.

KOREAN CUCUMBER SALAD

Prep Time: 10 mins - **Total Time:** 40 mins

SERVINGS: 10

NUTRITIONAL VALUE

Calories 117 kcal, Carbohydrates 15.8 g, Cholesterol 0 mg, Fat 6.1 g, Fiber 1.7 g, Protein 2.1 g, Sodium 1332 mg

INGREDIENTS

- three lbs. seedless cucumber, sliced paper- 1 tbsp. toasted sesame seeds thin
- 2 walnut halves, finely chopped(optional)
- 1 half tbsps. sea salt
- 1 clove garlic, minced
- half cup rice vinegar
- 1 half tsps. Korean red pepper powder
- 1 tbsp. rice wine
- freshly ground black pepper to taste
- 2 tbsps. sesame oil
- 2 tbsps. honey

- 2 tbsps. freshly squeezed lemon juice
- 1 green onion, sliced

DIRECTIONS

Step 1

Drain liquid from cucumbers after putting some sea salt by letting it stand for about 15 minutes and wrapping it in a paper towel to get more water out of it.

Step 2

Now combine rice vinegar, rice wine, honey, green onion, sesame seeds, lemon juice, walnuts, garlic, sesame oil, Korean red pepper powder and ground black pepper in a medium sized bowl.

Step 3

In this mixture, add cucumbers and refrigerate for at least 30 minutes after wrapping with plastic paper.

KIMCHEE JUN KIMCHEE PANCAKES

Prep Time: 15 mins - **Total Time:** 30 mins

SERVINGS: 8

NUTRITIONAL VALUE

Calories 199 kcal, Carbohydrates 26.5 g, Cholesterol 93 mg, Fat 7.1 g, Fiber 1.6 g, Protein 7.4 g, Sodium 513 mg

INGREDIENTS

- 1 cup kimchi, drained and chopped
- half tsp. Korean chili pepper flakes
- half cup reserved juice from kimchi
- (optional)
- 1 cup all-purpose flour

- half tsp. toasted sesame seeds
- 2 eggs
- (optional)
- 1 green onion, chopped
- 1 tbsp. vegetable oil
- salt to taste
- 1 tbsp. rice vinegar
- 1 tbsp. soy sauce
- half tsp. sesame oil

DIRECTIONS

Step 1

Combine kimchi, flour, eggs, kimchi juice and green onion in a medium sized bowl.

Step 2

Cook pancakes made from ¼ cup of batter in hot vegetable oil for about 5 minutes each side.

Step 3

Now combine rice vinegar, sesame oil, chili pepper flakes, soy sauce and toasted sesame seeds in a bowl and serve this with pancakes.

JAP CHAE GLASS NOODLES

Prep Time: 15 mins - **Total Time:** 20 mins

SERVINGS: 4

NUTRITIONAL VALUE

Calories 363 kcal, Carbohydrates 65.2 g, Cholesterol 0 mg, Fat 10.7 g, Fiber 0.6 g, Protein 1.9 g, Sodium 1073 mg

INGREDIENTS

- 1 pkg. (8 serving size) sweet potato
- three tbsps. vegetable oil
- vermicelli
- 1 tsp. toasted sesame seeds
- half cup reduced-sodium soy sauce
- 1/4 cup brown sugar
- half cup boiling water

DIRECTIONS

Step 1

Cover the vermicelli with hot water after cutting it into small pieces for 10 minutes and add a mixture of soy sauce, boiling water, and brown sugar into it.

Step 2

Cook this mixture in hot oil for about 5 minutes and just before serving, add noodles over it.

KONGNAMOOL **KOREAN SOYBEAN SPROUTS**

Prep Time: 10 mins - **Total Time:** 10 mins

SERVINGS: 4

NUTRITIONAL VALUE

Calories 376 kcal, Carbohydrates 21.4 g, Cholesterol 69 mg, Fat 21.9 g, Fiber 0.8 g, Protein 20.6 g, Sodium 1249 mg

INGREDIENTS

- 1 lb. soybean sprouts
- 2 tbsps. soy sauce

- 1/4 cup sesame oil
- 2 tbsps. Korean chili powder
- 1 half tsps. garlic, minced
- 2 tsps. sesame seeds
- 1/4 cup chopped green onion
- 2 tsps. rice wine vinegar, or to taste

DIRECTIONS

Step 1

Cook bean sprouts in salty boiling water for about 15 seconds and drain the water.

Step 2

Put sprouts in ice cold water for about three minutes to stop the cooking process and when these bean sprouts are cold, set them aside.

Step 3

Now combine soy sauce, sesame seeds, sesame oil and chili powder in a medium sized bowl and add bean sprouts to it.

Step 4

Now add some green onion and rice wine vinegar before refrigerating for some time.

Step 5

Serve

KOREAN BBQ SHORT RIBS(GALBI)

Prep Time: 20 mins - **Total Time:** 8 hrs

SERVINGS: 5

NUTRITIONAL VALUE

Calories 710 kcal, Fat 55.5 g, Carbohydrates 23.2g, Protein 28.8 g, Cholesterol 112 mg, Sodium 2231 mg

INGREDIENTS

- 3/4 C. soy sauce
- 1/2 large onion, minced
- 3/4 C. water
- 3 lbs Korean-style short ribs
- 3 tbsps white vinegar
- 1/4 C. dark brown sugar
- 2 tbsps white sugar
- 1 tbsp black pepper
- 2 tbsps sesame oil
- 1/4 C. minced garlic

DIRECTIONS

Step 1

Get a bowl, combine: vinegar, water, soy sauce, onion, brown sugar, garlic, regular sugar, sesame oil, and regular pepper.

Step 2

Add your ribs to this mix and cover the bowl with some plastic.

Step 3

Place the contents in the fridge overnight.

Step 4

Now grill the ribs for 6 mins per side on an oiled grate.

Step 5

Enjoy.

RED **PEPPER POTATOES**

Prep Time: 15 mins - **Total Time:** 35 mins

SERVINGS: 4

NUTRITIONAL VALUE

Calories 198 kcal, Carbohydrates 32.3 g, Cholesterol 0 mg, Fat 6.2 g, Fiber 5 g, Protein 4.6 , Sodium 352 mg

INGREDIENTS

- 1 half tbsps. soy sauce
- 1 pinch cayenne pepper, or to taste
- 1 half tbsps. vegetable oil
- three potatoes, cut into bite sized pieces
- 4 green onions, chopped
- 1 large red bell pepper, chopped
- 2 tsps. sesame seeds

DIRECTIONS

Step 1

Mix cayenne pepper and soy sauce in a bowl and cook potatoes over hot vegetable oil for about 5 minutes or until golden.

Step 2

Continue to cook for another minute after adding onion bell pepper and sesame seeds.

Step 3

Add soy sauce mixture and cook for another 3 minutes.

KOREAN **CRAB CAKES**

Prep Time: 15 mins - **Total Time:** 50 mins

SERVINGS: 4

NUTRITIONAL VALUE

Calories 254 kcal, Carbohydrates 9.6 g, Cholesterol 75 mg, Fat 17.4 g, Fiber 0.5 g, Protein 14.5 g, Sodium 620 mg

INGREDIENTS

- 1/4 cup mayonnaise
- salt and pepper to taste
- 2 tbsps. chopped fresh cilantro
- 1 half tbsps. peanut oil
- 1 tbsp. chopped fresh ginger
- 2 tsps. Asian fish sauce (nuoc mam or
- nam pla)
- 1 (6 ounce) can crabmeat - drained,
- flaked and cartilage removed
- three ounces chopped shrimp
- 1 half cups fresh breadcrumbs, made
- from crustless French bread

DIRECTIONS

Step 1

Combine crab, shrimp, bread crumbs, fresh ginger, mayonnaise, fish sauce and cilantro together in a bowl before adding salt and pepper.

Step 2

Take 1 fourth of a cup of this mixture and place in a bowl containing the remaining bread crumbs, and make a patty out of it.

Step 3

Do the same for the rest of the crab mixture.

Step 4

Now fry your patties in in hot oil over medium heat for about 5 minutes each side.

Step 5

Serve

KOREAN FIDDLEHEADS

Prep Time: 15 mins - **Total Time:** 30 mins

SERVINGS: 3

NUTRITIONAL VALUE

Calories 376 kcal, Carbohydrates 21.4 g, Cholesterol 69 mg, Fat 21.9 g, Fiber 0.8 g, Protein 20.6 g, Sodium 1249 mg

INGREDIENTS

- three cups fresh fiddlehead ferns, ends
- half tsp. black pepper
- trimmed
- 1 tbsp. fresh lemon juice
- three tbsps. unfiltered extra-virgin olive
- oil
- 1 clove garlic, minced
- half tsp. sea salt

DIRECTIONS

Step 1

Cook fiddlehead ferns in salty boiling water for about 10 minutes and drain the water.

Step 2

Add pepper, and garlic in some hot olive oil along with the ferns for about 5 minutes and remove everything from the heat and add lemon juice before serving.

BIBIMBAP **KOREAN VEGETABLE HOT POT**

Prep Time: 30 mins - **Total Time:** 50 mins

SERVINGS: 3

NUTRITIONAL VALUE

Calories 395 kcal, Fat 18.8 g, Carbohydrates 45g, Protein 13.6 g, Cholesterol 196 mg, Sodium 1086 mg

INGREDIENTS

- 2 tbsps sesame oil
- 2 tbsps soy sauce
- 1 C. carrot matchsticks
- 1/4 tsp ground black pepper
- 1 C. zucchini matchsticks
- 1 tbsp butter
- 1/2 (14 oz.) can bean sprouts, drained
- 3 eggs
- 6 oz. canned bamboo shoots, drained

- 3 tsps sweet red chili sauce, or to
- 1 (4.5 oz.) can sliced mushrooms, taste drained
- 1/8 tsp salt to taste
- 2 C. cooked and cooled rice
- 1/3 C. sliced green onions

DIRECTIONS

Step 1

Stir fry your zucchini and carrots and in sesame oil for 7 mins then add in: mushrooms, bamboo, and sprouts.

Step 2

Stir fry the mix for 7 more mins then add in some salt and remove the veggies from the pan.

Step 3

Add in: black pepper, rice, soy sauce, and green onions. And get everything hot.

Step 4

Now in another pan fry your eggs in butter. When the yolks are somewhat runny but the egg whites are cooked place the eggs to the side. This should take about 3 mins of frying.

Step 5

Layer an egg on some rice.

Step 6

Add the veggies on top of the egg and some red chili sauce over everything.

Step 7

Enjoy.

KOREAN CASHEW HUMMUS

Prep Time: 5 mins - **Total Time:** 5 mins

SERVINGS: 3

NUTRITIONAL VALUE

Calories 270 kcal, Carbohydrates 28.6 g, Cholesterol 0 mg, Fat 16.5 g, Fiber 3 g, Protein 7.8 g,Sodium 367 mg

INGREDIENTS

- 2 cups corn kernels, thawed if frozen
- 1/4 tsp. onion powder
- 1 cup cashews
- 1/4 tsp. garlic powder
- 1 tsp. lemon juice, or more to taste
- 1/4 tsp. salt

DIRECTIONS

Step 1

Place everything mentioned in a blender and blend it for about 1 minute.

Step 2

Serve with rice.

BULGOGI KOREAN CHICKEN STIR FRY

Prep Time: 15 mins - **Total Time:** 30 mins

SERVINGS: 4

NUTRITIONAL VALUE

Calories 269 kcal, Fat 11.6 g, Carbohydrates 13.2g, Protein 27.5 g, Cholesterol 69 mg, Sodium 1230 mg

INGREDIENTS

- 1/4 C. diced onion
- salt and ground black pepper to taste
- 5 tbsps soy sauce
- 1 lb skinless, boneless chicken breasts, cut into 2 1/2 tbsps brown sugar
- thin strips
- 2 tbsps minced garlic
- 2 tbsps sesame oil
- 1 tbsp sesame seeds
- 1/2 tsp cayenne

DIRECTIONS

Step 1

Get a bowl, combine: black pepper, onions, salt, brown sugar, soy sauce, cayenne, garlic, sesame seeds, and sesame oils.

Step 2

Add in your chicken to the mix and stir the mix before pouring everything in a wok.

Step

Stir fry the contents until your chicken is fully done for about 17 mins.

Step 4

Enjoy.

KOREAN **WHOLE CHICKEN**

Prep Time: 10 mins - **Total Time:** 50 mins

SERVINGS: 4

NUTRITIONAL VALUE

Calories 794 kcal, Fat 54.7 g, Carbohydrates 6g, Protein 65.3 g, Cholesterol 1255 mg, Sodium 1338 mg

INGREDIENTS

- 1 (3 lb) whole chicken, meat remove
- 1 tbsp white sugar
- from the bones, slices in the 1/8" thick
- 1 tsp monosodium glutamate (MSG)
- square pieces
- 1/4 C. soy sauce
- 2 tbsps sesame seeds
- 1/8 tsp salt
- 1/8 tsp ground black pepper
- 1 green onion, minced
- 1 clove garlic, minced
- 1 tsp peanut oil

DIRECTIONS

Step 1

Combine your cut chicken with some soy sauce in a bowl.

Step 2

Now toast your sesame seeds in a pan.

Step 3

Once they begin to pop place them in a bowl and top the seeds with salt.

Step 4

Now mash the seeds with a big wooden spoon and add in: MSG, pepper, sugar, onions, oil, and garlic.

Step 5

Now combine both bowls and let the chicken sit in the sesame mix for 35 mins.

Step 6

Begin to stir fry your chicken in the same pan for 2 mins before placing a cover on the pot and cooking until the meat is fully done.

Step 7

Enjoy.

KOREAN VEGETABLES

Prep Time: 20 mins - **Total Time:** 40 mins

SERVINGS: 6

NUTRITIONAL VALUE

Calories 106 kcal, Fat 4.9 g, Carbohydrates 14g, Protein 4 g, Cholesterol 0 mg, Sodium 1225 mg

INGREDIENTS

- 5 medium zucchini, sliced
- 2 tbsps sesame oil
- 1 bunch green onions, sliced

ground black pepper to taste

- 1/4 C. white vinegar
- 1/2 C. soy sauce
- 1/4 C. water
- 2 tbsps sugar

DIRECTIONS

Step 1

Add the following to a big pot: sesame oil, zucchini, sugar, green onions, water, vinegar, and soy sauce.

Step 2

Add in some black pepper as well.

Step 3

Stir everything, then place a lid on the pot.

Step 4

Let the contents cook with a low level of heat for about 22 mins until the veggies are soft.

Step 5

Enjoy.

www.ingramcontent.com/pod-product-compliance
Lightning Source LLC
LaVergne TN
LVHW082248150826
845677LV00009B/1570

* 9 7 9 8 4 4 6 0 4 8 5 9 5 *